Bound To Myself

Rebecca Payne

BookLeaf Publishing

India | USA | UK

Presentation by *BookLeaf Publishing*

Web: www.bookleafpub.com

E-mail: info@bookleafpub.com

ISBN: 9789357446174

First edition 2022

DEDICATION

Dedicated to my friends and family, thank you for sticking by me through so much.

Your Eyes

Your eyes are the ones I want to see,
The ones I wish to stare at everyday, every
conversation, every silent moment.
The eyes are the window to the soul as some say,
and your soul is pure and bright.
I'll never admit it to you though, that your eyes
are in my dreams keeping me calm and content.
Maybe one day, your eyes will be all I will see.

High

My breath is unsteady
As I ignite the flame
Trying to calm my breath
Before doing it again
The look of blood shot eyes staring back at me
I breath out, and light the substance in the night
I breathe in deeply, deeper than last
Breathing out the smoke to forget, the troubles
of the days past

Home

Home is dark,
Home is pretending there is light when we are
all just peering through the shadows
Trying to catch a glimpse of those nearby.
Home is dampness,
The cold and musty smells entering my nose
when least expected.
Home is retreating my safe space,
Even though that space is just as dark and damp
as the rest of the house. Where I can't find my
light, or happiness.

Home is dark. And I can't wait to find my light.

Weakness

What is your biggest weakness?
Is a common question at an interview

My biggest weakness?

It's thinking I'm not enough
I'm never good enough
I'm too odd to be loved
I'm too strange to be accepted

But instead, I say,
I can become unfocused sometimes

Unfocused on my moral grounds and believing
all the negatives
But they won't know that part
They'll accept it, and continue on

Clueless to the facts laid out on the table like
tarot cards revealing my future
My biggest weakness, is being unfocused.

Will It Go Away?

One friend gained, and a "friend" lost.
This is my path and I'll walk it no matter the
cost.
The life lessons for me still ache my heart
Though, Allah knows what I'll do long before I
know
So I take comfort in knowing He has a plan for
me.
A plan for someone who has always felt weak,
alone, lost and confused.
I still those though.
I wonder when it'll go away.

Punchline

Getting over you will be the easiest thing I do.
Why? Because you beat to the punchline.
That's all you did.
I'm ready to move on because I'm stronger than
ever.
Have a happy life because it won't be a long one.
No ever lives for a long time.

Alone

It's all nothing
The fan on my skin
The music in my ears
The phone in my hand

The light in my eyes are gone,
I am gone,
I am nothing but a husk of who I once was.

Damage is the only way to feel,
The only way to understand,
Understand why I'm so... Alone

The Stars

I told the stars about you,
Oh how brightly they shone,
For every word make them glow brighter than
ever before.
But you never spoke about me,
Never returned the adoration,
And so the darkness swallowed them whole.

How?

How?
How can I love you so deeply and you'll never
know?
How can I make you see how I feel without
having to fall?
How can you be the one but so far out of reach?
How can you be the one?
The one that'll never be mine.

I'm not okay.

It always hits the hardest when you're happy.
When you're smiling and laughing, it creeps
back in.
The snide remarks in your ears about what your
friends are thinking about you.
Always. Happens.
I don't want to pretend I'm okay anymore, but I
have to.

You Make Me Feel

How do you do it?
Make me feel?

The way you talk and laugh, the way you light
up a room with just your presence alone.
You make me feel,
Feel happy,
No longer numb.

No longer wishing for the sweet relief of death.

Until you go,
You pull away from my grasp again, I feel you
slip away from me once more.

Let me help you feel,
Help you feel the same way you make me feel.

Of Brilliant Fireflies

The way they light up the sky,
The shimmer of their glow on the face of the
lake.

The graceful deer watching as they take sip of
the crisp water,
The stunning Fey that sit by idly, awaiting for a
new human to approach them.

The tales of brilliant fireflies draws one in again
this fateful night,
Another deal struck, another promise made.

Of brilliant fireflies, should there be more to
pay.

Life Beneath the Universe

The stars shine brightly, the moon sits high,
Waiting for more passerby, to relish in the
moonlights glow,
To wonder what life is like, out in the Universe
above.

While those within space, travelling the traverse,
wonder what it's like,
On the ever glowing planet, the place where
flora and fauna bloom, while the humans there
destroy it one year at a time,
Sometimes they too, wonder what life like,
beneath they Universe they know.

I crave

I crave the days that I thought I would have you
in my arms.
I never got to meet you, tell anyone about you.
I never got to celebrate a life I had created.
Because you left before you could bloom, yet
you planted your little seed in my brain.
And so forever I will hold the love for you, my
little baby that I never got to know.

Tight-rope

I was on the final line of my rope and now it's
snapped.
What do I do now?
The more I grab at each strand to tie it back
together like I have many times before,
The more it disintegrates into nothing more.
The fraying lines burning my calloused hands
again.
The panic sets in, my chest is tight and my eyes
are wet with the uncertainty I'll get out.
I was on the final line of my rope,
And I'm trapped.

Sleep

The nights grow colder,
The blankets pile up.
My eyelids have been heavy all day, unable to
stay open, to stay attentive.
But come night, warm in my bed, with the
blankets piled up, they're wide open.
Ready to face the day that's already gone.
The sleep I so crave is gone, and it's another
sleepless night.

How many hours has it been?

Orchids

The orchids are white,
Ones as white as ghost are rare.
They're pure white, just like your hair.

Your eyes, as stunning as they be, pierce into my
soul,
To read all that can be seen.

The fables are true, the ones you call Fey, are the
ones who are true.
The deals they make, cannot come undone, for
once they're made, you cannot hide.

And so I sit, under the Jacaranda tree, sipping
my tea, and loving on thee.
The Fey that I met one fateful night, who I now
live with, a life where I cannot run.

Love Hurts Sometimes

I just need you,
You make me happy, smile, feel all giddy inside.
Yeah, I just need you.

But you'll never know, why would I be so bold?
To let you know that I've given you a piece of
me.

That you'll throw away once you know?
So best to keep it to myself to know.

Immortal Love

The treasures you gave me over the years, I've
kept every single one.
I must have thousands now.
A long with the millions of memories.
The first kisses, hugs, hello, and the goodbyes.

The goodbyes are never easy. I've seen your face
a million times over, shaping into someone I
knew I'd lose.
I didn't want to lose you again.
The sad tale of the immortal and the mortal
never seems to come to a happy ending.
How could it?
All the new and exciting and different and
unfortunate versions of you keep be hopeful that
one day, after a million more, or even now, I get
to spend the rest of my life with you.

This time, I see your sleeping figure, so content
and restful. The youthful glow still in your face,
oh how I'd miss you.
Until the next time.

Thunder cracks now, startling you awake but as
always, I comfort you. You've always been

afraid of the thunder. I always can "guess" your favourite food and drinks to your surprise.
I hold you close, kissing your temple sweetly.

The years of heartache I hold within me is bubbling. It's leaking over the brim and I can't stop.
Oh how I'll miss you. I can't lose you again. I want to make a million memories where you know them too.
Why can't I just be blessed with your kisses forever.

The way you kiss my nose, then my cheeks, my forehead and lastly my lips, peppering them sweetly and so pure.
The way you cup my face, running your thumbs over my flushed face, wiping away the tears that seem never ending. How can you look so understanding without knowing what I mean?

Until that time comes, I'll hold you dear to my heart. I'll kiss you sweetly, I'll love our lives together.

And so the time has come, we're under the weeping willow, as always. This solom place, keeps bringing us back here. Your face, though aged is still ever so perfect to me. I'll kiss you,

rubbing your cheeks from the tears as you once
did mine, and your final breath is bitter sweet.
I know I'll meet you again my love, but the pain
never ceases once you're gone.

And so I find you again, the first hello, the first
kiss and the first time you fall in love with me,
I'll never forget these. Ever. Never for another
century and those after.
I promise one day we will meet again and I'll be
able to tell you the memories I have of us, while
watching the sunrise, and I won't have to say
goodbye anymore. Please universe, let me find
them one last time and keep them forever.
Please.

Fire

The fire is warm at my feet.
Comforting as I hear the crackles of the wood splitting, the crumbling ashy wood falling from it's place on the log it once was.
The book in my hands was old yet new to me. The crinkly pages, the smell of ink and slight dust invading my nose with each page I turn. Enveloped with the information within. The strange softness to the pages despite the age, how well it's been used, the love and care placed into each letter in each word. The details within each drawing and sketch.
The coarse leather in my hand as I balance the book, taking a sip of my once hot tea, I grimace as the cold liquid reaches my tongue. Placing the cup down I run my fingers across the page as I read, the slight tickle in my finger tips as I do so.

My brain just wont figure out the words that make it nice, leaving the solitary word to lay on the page waiting for me to continue. It may never know what it was meant to become because I cannot convey the message it so desperately needs to be a great story.

Words

And as she sat at her desk, laptop in front of her,
The words longing to be written, flowing from
her fingertips onto the screen,
She knows she's done her most, that she has
done her best for the time being.

And she knows, that despite the troubles of her
life, the trials to get to where she is today, her
written words speak volumes more than her
spoken ones ever could.